Jürgen Mann

AF156498

Princess Abbey

I had to write this book as of the
unexpected events last year!

Jürgen Mann

Princess Abbey

The fantastic dream of my dog`s life was
challenged last year

Jürgen Mann, born in Sondershausen/Thuringia, escaped in 1961 from East- to West-Germany and worked many years in the international business environment. Since a few years, he and his wife Linda are proud owners of a Havanese female dog. Today they live in Upper Franconia in Germany.

Hello to all of you, here I am again! It has been quite a while since I wrote to you – and I feel that it is necessary to tell you all about what has happened last year. Not everything was pleasant!

Last year was eventful and to make it clear, I do not want this ever to happen to me again!

What a drama!

First of all, here is one of my photos Daddy took recently. I am now almost eleven years old or in human life: I am 80 now! But I am still fit – again!

But let`s start from the beginning. It was in January last year. Daddy and I went for a walk around the usual path in Wildenberg. The sun was out and of course, it was a bit cold. But you know: I like it cool! There were also a few patches of snow left. I love to smell snow or go walking in it!

Every time a car comes and opens the doors, I am curious if some of my friends might jump out. So, there is a white station wagon coming and I went to the back, sat down and waited. The owner opened the back door – and a crazy wild Jack Russel jumped out and bit me right in the neck! He did not let go, his sharp teeth went through my skin and I was screaming my heart out! The bad thing is that when they bite you, pulling them away is dangerous as the sharp teeth can rip the wound even bigger! And this bad dog did not let go until the owner hit him hard.

You can imagine, not only was I surprised but shocked and I was hurt so badly, Daddy too! Horrible!

Finally, Daddy could take me up and carried me back to the car to go home and check the wound with Mommy. The owner got Daddy`s name and phone number and apologized.

Yeah, right, he should have taken his dog on a short lease!

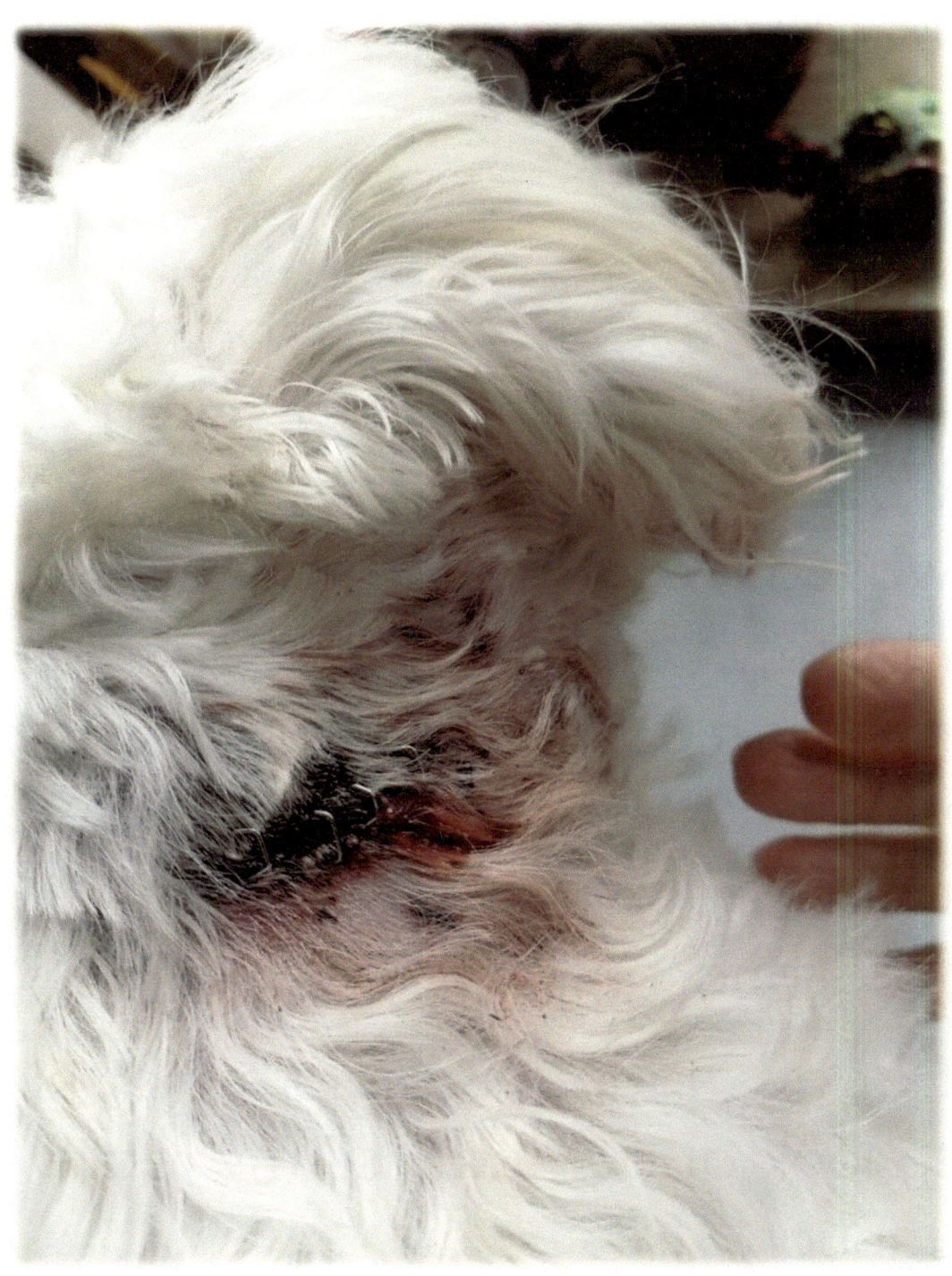

He called Daddy later but did not leave his name - and the phone number was blocked! Terrible, he should pay for all my upcoming medical bills!

When we got home Mommy was terrified! She tried to wash the wound and we called the clinic; it was Saturday afternoon, a problem. Mommy and Daddy thought it might be good to wait a day but this was wrong as we found out. Vets are seldom available on the weekend, not good.

Daddy made this picture; not nice to look at but this was my reality in January!

Well, we finally went on Sunday to have my wound checked. They thought that stapeling it might be enough – wrong! A day later we checked the bite again: it got badly infected! We decided that a proper operation would be the best. This bite needed to be taken care of as soon as possible! It hurt me but I am tough and I did not cry.

Why did this happen to me?

I can tell you that I was terrified and stressed out for about three days. I could not believe that another dog would bite me. I am so nice and cute and so friendly!

Three days later we went to the clinic again for the operation and they gave me a novicane shot, also not good but necessary. Mommy and Daddy were worried as a novicane shot could also leave me with long term problems.

Well, it took the doctor over one hour to fix my wound and sew it tight!

My parents waited outside and got worried. Finally, the nurses carried me out in their arms and layed me down on a blanket. As soon as I woke up, Mommy and Daddy took me to the car; they brought my favorite basket and layed me in it as comfortably as possible.

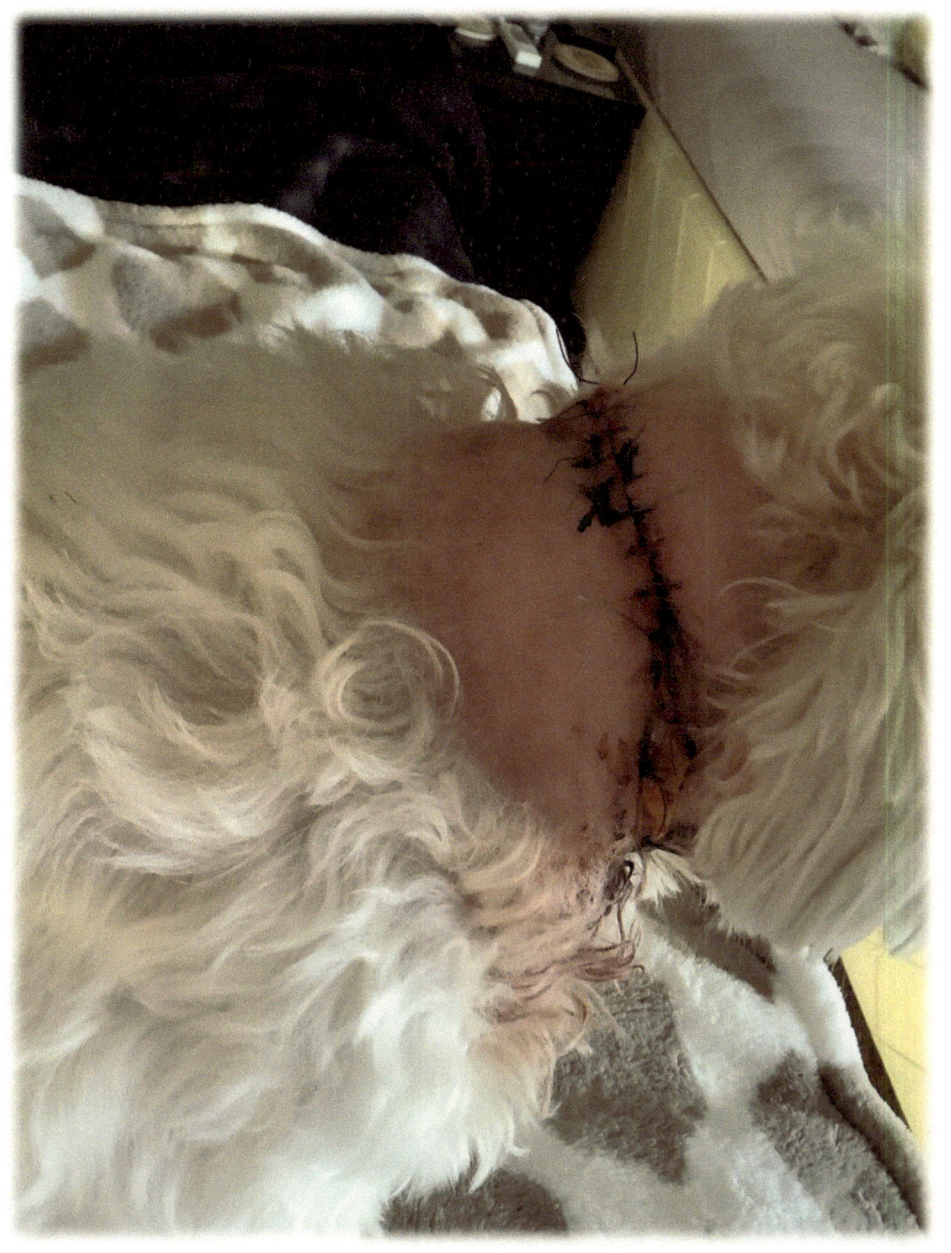

The scar looked terrible but it was sewn perfectly and today you cannot see it!

I needed a few days rest! My wound did not look too nice with all the stitches and the shaved neck!

I just wanted to sleep!

I was hoping that everything would work out for me!

And of course, Mommy and Daddy will take care of me until I am totally healed!

After the operation the scar needed about four weeks until it looked a bit better and my fur was starting to grow over it. At this time, they took out the stitches in the wound. I have to say that I was strong and felt almost normal again after about two months.

Thanks to Mommy and Daddy and all the angels in heaven, I survived this horrible drama!

We went to the vet several times for a check-up, everything was going well! On the way there, there is a McDonald`s restaurent. Did I ever tell you that I love Hamburgers?

But only those from Mc Donald`s.

They make them extra for me without any spices as this would not be good for my tummy. Daddy orders these burger patties especially for me: not one, but three!

And here is another surprise: they allow dogs to come in and eat in the restaurent! Unbelievable – at least for my American friends.

I always enjoy these Hamburgers!

My neck healed wonderfully well, I was so glad! But then something else happened!

In the middle of June, my right eye started to be infected: the corner turned totally red, my eye also seemed to be swolen! Not that I could not see but something was definitely wrong!

Our doctors in the clinic recommended that we drive to Nuremberg to an eye specialist.

We did it the coming week. He could not do anything, just did an ultrasonic examine and wanted us to do an MRI!

Fortunately, there was a female vet doctor near our town who he knew and who had the MRI equipment for animals. She had a very good reputation and we were hoping that she would find out what is wrong with my eye. It looked like a simple infection but who knew.

This certainly would mean another procedure with novicane! Not good but again necessary!

Well, we went there for a first consultation; she was very nice and we made an appointment for the MRI. Mommy and Daddy just wanted to make sure that there is nothing behind the eye like a tumor.

Or could it be related to the bite in the neck five months ago?

Two weeks later I had my MRI. Eye drops, infusion and novicane – what I had to go through! But I am tough!

After a good hour, they brought me out and we needed to wait for another hour as they give you some infusion to protect you from drying out.

But the most important news was: there is nothing really wrong with my eye!!! Okay, I could not blink very well but the nerves causing it could heal over time. I take vitamin B12 twice a day; Mommy and Daddy call them Candy. They taste okay. In addition, I get some eye-drops.

Now after about 8 months, the eye and blinking is better, not 100% but much better. At night, I can close my eye totally, blinking is still a bit off.

We went for a check-up last week; our vet was very pleased with the healing!

The vet lady also recommended a teeth clean! Oh my god, another procedure! We got some tooth paste and Mommy is brushing my teeth now more regularly. I do not like this and I hate the paste!

It is not fun getting old!

Well, life goes on: we now have winter and a lot of snow. Yes, the country looks pretty!

You know that my second nature is being a polar bear: I love the snow! And temperatures in the twenties do not bother me.

On the other hand, I am getting a bit older now and digging the snow like a plow, as I used to, is pretty tireing!

Therefore, my walks are not as long as they were years ago.

Still, I enjoy walking with my parents and see some of my friends sometimes!

Before I close, I have to tell you about a few new behaviours I developed.

Morning routines are still the same with „hide and seek" some goodies, now.a.days my candy pill and then walk with Daddy. Then a good nap on Mommy`s bed. Then lunch with my parents – if Mommy cooked something which tastes yummy to me. Then another walk and another nap – nothing new so far. But my evenings have changed!

In winter, we get visitors: to make it clear, I do not like invaders in my garden.

First, there is this strange gray cat that we do not know from where it is coming. But it is hungry and eats the food Mommy puts in the porch bowl. It is not my favorite food but sometimes, I eat it so this cat does not get it!

Secretly, Mommy refills the bowl. I am laying then in front of the porch door and watch until the cat comes – and I will have a fit and bark so it runs away.

Then Mommy takes me away until the kitty comes back and eats.

Too bad, I would have chased it!

The other visitors we have during the winter is a deer family: Mommy- and Daddy-dear and two kids. They are hungry! They are coming from the forest down and are obviously not too shy to eat the oatmeal Mommy puts out. I hear them coming and bark. Mommy has to hide me in the front room until they leave. I do not like this but I think it is okay.

They need to have some food in their belly!

Oh, and then it is dinner time for me! I like it when I am fed piece by piece and by hand from Daddy. It is nice to be pampered! Therefore Daddy feeds me my dinner – one little piece after another one. I like it. These are the hard little bites; the second course are treats and then my evening candy pill. I like this procedure.

Daddy says that I am eating like the Romans did: laying down.

And then it is night time – on my own bed! I need this good night sleep!

After all, I am happy to have survived this year and to tell you the truth: I am definitely looking forward to a year without bad events - and so far it looks pretty good.

I am curious what the future holds. As soon as there are new things to report, I will get back to you in any case!

Take care and stay healthy!
Sincerely,

Your Abbey

© 2023 Jürgen Mann
Production and publishing:
BoD - Books on Demand, Norderstedt
ISBN: 978-3-7347-2868-6

FSC
www.fsc.org

MIX

Papier aus ver-
antwortungsvollen
Quellen
Paper from
responsible sources

FSC® C105338